THE MIDDLE

ALSO BY STEPHEN COLLIS

Poetry

Anarchive
*The Commons**
Decomp (with Jordan Scott)
Mine
*On the Material**
*A History of the Theories of Rain**
*Once in Blockadia**
*To the Barricades**

Fiction

The Red Album

Non-Fiction

*Almost Islands: Phyllis Webb and the Pursuit of the Unwritten**
*Dispatches from the Occupation: A History of Change**
*Phyllis Webb and the Common Good: Poetry / Anarchy / Abstraction**
Through Words of Others: Susan Howe and Anarcho-Scholasticism

As Editor

*A Dream in the Eye: The Complete Paintings and Collages of Phyllis Webb**
Reading Duncan Reading: Robert Duncan and the Poetics of Derivation
    (with Graham Lyons)
Taking Measures: Selected Serial Poems, by George Bowering*

* Published by Talonbooks

THE MIDDLE

POEMS

STEPHEN COLLIS

TALONBOOKS

© 2024 Stephen Collis

Talonbooks
9259 Shaughnessy Street, Vancouver, British Columbia, Canada V6P 6R4
talonbooks.com

Talonbooks is located on xʷməθkʷəy̓əm, Sḵwx̱wú7mesh, and səlilwətaɬ Lands.

First printing: 2024

Typeset in Arno
Printed and bound in Canada on 100% post-consumer recycled paper

Cover photograph by Stephen Collis

Talonbooks acknowledges the financial support of the Canada Council for the Arts, the Government of Canada through the Canada Book Fund, and the Province of British Columbia through the British Columbia Arts Council and the Book Publishing Tax Credit.

Library and Archives Canada Cataloguing in Publication

Title: The middle : poems / Stephen Collis
Names: Collis, Stephen, 1965- author.
Identifiers: Canadiana 20240386450 | ISBN 9781772016420 (softcover)
Subjects: LCGFT: Ecopoetry. | LCGFT: Poetry.
Classification: LCC PS8555.O4938 M53 2024 | DDC C811/.54—dc23

For Cathy, lucky to be stuck in the middle with you

a tree is always an immutable
traveller

—ETEL ADNAN

The middle of the road is trying to find me.

—THE PRETENDERS

All I want to do is sit on my ass all day and fart and think of Dante.

—SAMUEL BECKETT

PREFACE

Every state of being contains a story of
motion waiting to be told.

—JENNY ERPENBECK

The deep middleness of things compels me – this fraught stretch of life between certain pasts (let's recall, if only a few, colonial land grabs, empires in their always-new clothes, vast carbon incinerations) and uncertain futures (can we yet dream of a time when all will come to have a relationship to the earth that is welcoming and mutually sustaining?). I am writing this in a winged hut at the back of my mind, which is to say deep in an imaginary forest (where there are no actual trees) – a place I find whenever I'm surrounded by books and silence. That's a middle of things that necessarily feels like respite, an eddy in the flow, as opposed to the middleness that feels like a slow-motion tumbling – *in medias res* – as the planet tips, and the turtle sloughs all that's been built off its back.

According to Nabokov, life is just a crack of light in the middle of two eternities of darkness. I think the middle is not the still centre of a turning world, not fulcrum, but the active and tensed dialectical space created by the energy of polarized opposites, within which we all move, pushed pulled driven and desiring. The middle is thus a space of almost perpetual mobility, where the go-between goes between – as well as the space of possibility (where we could still change direction and arrive elsewhere, elsewhen). But we all know that the middle is not nearly as sexy as either End Times or New Dawns. Middlebrow. Middling talent. The middle of the road. Stuck in the middle with you. One should avoid changing horses midstream or sitting on a fence too long, and a centrist, I've often thought, is the worst possible thing: the politically indecisive middle of ideological nowhere. But middles are not centres – they are too shifty, too fluid, too fraught and entangled for that. To be in the middle is to be in relation, moving between. When it is declared that we are now "post" any given concept or condition, what is really going on is that what we are in the middle of, what we are moving through, has been recognized at last. The "post" is a sighting of the far shore towards which we might be moving, a moment where it becomes possible to triangulate our current position. We are perhaps with Dante and Virgil, on the shores of the Stygian lake, Canto VII of the *Inferno*, as depicted by William Blake.

William Blake, *Dante and Virgil on the Edge of the Stygian Pool (from Dante's "Divine Comedy")*, Harvard Art Museums/Fogg Museum, Bequest of Grenville L. Winthrop, Photo © President and Fellows of Harvard College, 1943.658

I don't want to be too bleak. Really. Despair I know is easy to give in to and I'd like to find my way back to something more ... committed. The doors to something else swing open and close again constantly, somewhere on a windy hill, middle of wherever it is you are, a moth making its way in the wind at dusk towards some distant light, or a bee clinging to a flower in the storm. I put the largest fears, the daily despairs I find around the house, into poems, like encasing radioactive waste in a lead sarcophagus, or deep in an empty salt mine. I want to be realistically idealistic, or idealistically realistic. There's no preserving or conserving *the way things were* anymore – that boat has sailed, with a bunch of rich people on board, their plastic-and-chrome environments polished and encrypted, zipped and cached. Everything and everyone's on the move actually, even those who don't know they are in motion yet. Movements happen at different speeds – but we are all nonetheless on the move, and I think we need to help each other along – the more ably winged and quick-legged taking up the more fixedly rooted ones in our arms. As it were.

This long poem grown from the middle of life comes in three parts. The first finds its seeds in the assembling of a small library of Robin Blaser's books – a decade after the poet's death, his books arrived at the university where I work, like a long-whispered echo through the trees. So I ran through the Holy Forest like a madman – there was some urgency, the librarians said – so I ran, pulling quotations from volumes like branches broken from the trees, apples caught as they fell. Storms were coming – heavy rains on deforested hillsides, fried by fire weather and summer forest fires (past which Cathy and I drove – the sides of the highway engulfed in flame – in the summer of 2021) and excessive logging, threatening flood – indeed, it was an *atmospheric river* that November, shaking and drenching Burnaby Mountain where I wrote. And the poets seemed to be washing away with the soils of the treeless mountainsides. First Phyllis Webb and Lee Maracle, on a

Remembrance Day to remember, and then just days later, Etel Adnan. In a lashed province, in a small study I had assembled on a mountain, Blaser's marginalia led me to make a music of fire and flood, some underworld songs for the beloved dead, a poem of mourning and a prayer for the return of the trees. Time was of the – of its – essence. It was another sketch of a poem, open and potentially unending, that I would not have to have written, in futures imperfect.

I had thought that was it. But then a quotation found in a review of a new translation of Dante sent me seeking: "It's the middle section of *Purgatory* that speaks most directly to the self-inflicted wounds of our present condition," Robert Pogue Harrison writes. Where *Inferno* and *Paradiso* are realms of fixity and stasis (time does not pass, and everyone has their final place of either torment or bliss), in *Purgatorio* all is in motion and no one remains, as Teodolinda Barolini writes in *The Undivine Comedy* (another of Blaser's books), "In *Purgatorio* all the intersecting lifelines are in motion, voyaging in time – just as on earth all parties in any encounter are moving forward along their respective lines of becoming." There are other things I might note here – that Dante himself was living a refugee's life, exiled from his home in Florence, the whole time he was writing the *Commedia*, that his entire three-part poem begins with the words "In the middle" (*Nel mezzo*), and that *Purgatorio* is where the poet expresses "a love of the planet and everything that makes it our cosmic home" (Harrison). But the key thing was that – aiming at the *middle* of the middle, and so taking only the middle lines from the tercets of Dante's middle canticle – I heard the desperate and vibrating voices of migrants striving for the shore, the search for refuge in strange lands, that spoke to the heart of the work I had been involved in, for the better part of a decade, with Refugee Tales – an annual walk in solidarity with refugees, asylum seekers, and those with lived experience of immigration detention. Jacques Le Goff, in *The Birth of Purgatory*, writes that "Sentences to Purgatory were not indefinite; they had fixed terms," which is not the case with indefinite immigration detention in the UK, so the comparison is not exact, but rather felt, intuited, glimpsed out of the corner of the eye. And yet the moment of pilgrims' arrival on the shore, the light of hope cast across the sea, the climb in search of the earthly paradise, the memories of loss and separation each pilgrim soul carries with them – all this resonates with today's refugee experience.

It also mattered that I wrote this poem with my sister Gail's voice in my ear, in the autumn of the twentieth year since her passing – Dante a key link between us, dating from a 1993 workshop we took together on "The Divine Comedy as the Soul's Journey" (I know) – she a Beatrice figure that has long kept me climbing, challenging *mala condotta*, aware that *l'amor è il seme in te*. Perhaps, as Vivek Narayanan writes, "*Every* translation is a hoax" – certainly I am a pretender, working my way back and forth between the *Purgatorio*s of D.M. Black and W.S. Merwin – with a few of my own digressions and faulty translations thrown somewhere in the middle.

The third part, which quickly followed the second, came back to Blaser's books – or to one book in particular: his copy of Paul Friedrich's *Proto-Indo-European Trees: The Arboreal System of a Prehistoric People*, bearing the trace of Blaser's light pencil, its pages interleaved with slips of paper marking important passages. The book engages its investigation of the hypothetical ancient root language via its descendant tree names, mapped onto the pollen record to note where and when such names perhaps came into use. It thus reconstructs a lost language tree by following the climatological movements of various arboreal species: linguistics on top of paleobotany, climate change and the wanderings of people and trees, both in step with their warming and cooling worlds, whispering one to another. I took a ride on a raft of seed-dispersal research, and a journey into a realm of treeless and ancient mountains in Wales, in the company of several other poets, became this poem's major pilgrimage. The final touches were put on the poem in the village of Fairbourne, low on the coast between Eryri and Barmouth Bay, a village about to be swallowed by the rising seas.

The Middle is thus a long poem made up of three separate but linked long poems – each taking up a different mode of making-long: the serial or musical suite ("Sketch of a Poem I Will Not Have Written:

Blazing Space"), the procedural, numbered sequence of cantos ("The Middle"), and the long narrative poem (as "Gardens in Motion" gradually becomes). Each poem finds itself somewhere on a mountain, in the company of trees, or the ghosts of now-absent trees, climbing in altitude or heading north, in search, perhaps, of lost earthly paradises. And this book, too, itself forms the middle part of a trilogy of books on our climatic moment – call it *Sketch of a Poem I Will Not Have Written* – begun with *A History of the Theories of Rain*, and to be continued in a book entitled *Terminalia* (destination unknown). I once imagined I was writing an endless, borderless poem called "The Barricades Project," the themes of which were revolution and change; maybe I still am, but the themes are now catastrophe and time – and mobility – which are the shadow companions of those earlier themes. I discover where I am from the middle, not the beginning or the end. Even when a long poem aspires to include everything, as Rachel Blau DuPlessis notes, it only manages to be "all middle." We are all between climates now, diasporic seed scatterers on our way somewhere else, residents of a mobile middle I'm trying not to mind singing my way through.

⚜

Today we are in the middle of the complete redistribution of life on earth: all planetary life is currently in motion, fleeing the rising heat, heading north or south, towards the poles, at measurable rates (as far as fauna are concerned, on average, seventeen kilometres per decade on land, seventy-two by sea). Mammals, fish, crustaceans, reptiles, rodents, birds, insects, plants, grasses, trees – everything. I think the only ethical response is to enable, rather than resist, this total mobility – in all its varied sociobiotic forms. I am drawn to human-plant relations in part because they form the less obvious partnership in mobility – although as Stefano Mancuso writes, "When it comes to migrants and migration, it is helpful to study plants in order to understand that we are talking about an unstoppable phenomenon." Plants move, as ecologist Louis

Pitelka has it, "by creep of root and shower of seed," but half of all plant species rely on animals to disperse their seeds. Due to human intervention, plants have already lost 60 percent of their capacity to track climate change globally due to "defaunation" – the loss of the animals within whose guts and knotted fur they used to ride. And this in a context where many plant species need to shift hundreds and sometimes thousands of metres per year to track their climate niche, which is steadily shifting poleward.

French gardener Gilles Clément writes of the "Planetary Garden": "The feeling of ecological finiteness makes the limits of the biosphere appear like the enclosure of living beings." Clément is working with the etymology of the word "garden" here, which like "paradise" means an "enclosure" or "walled space": the enclosure of the planet, then, refers to the absolute biospheric limits we have reached – "ecological finiteness," in his terms – and which define what many are calling the Anthropocene. If the entire planet is now enclosed, why would the gardener not approach it as one vast garden? This creates, for Clément, an opportunity "to work with (rather than against) the powerful flux of life," provoking him to imagine a kind of utopian ecology "where all of life together, including humanity, interacts without borders" – and where every true garden is a garden in motion (*le jardin en mouvement*). Clément refers to mobile plants as "vagabonds" which decamp to abandoned zones that he calls "undocumented" tracts. He also calls these abandoned zones a "Third Landscape:" "a territory for the many species that cannot find a place elsewhere." Such spaces – which we have often called "wastes" and which are characterized by a dereliction that speaks at once of both "ruin" and "development" – are everywhere humans have been: "The borders of the Third Landscape are the borders of the Planetary Garden, the limits of the biosphere."

What can we do but get out of the way at last. Make space. Create migration corridors. Leave alone so the natural world can adjust and expand once again. Let people and plants reach the shore, climb the mountain. In Clément's "Manifesto of the Third Landscape," this is exactly what the planetary gardener suggests: "Design a wide and permeable network of land. Create as many gateways as necessary for communication between them." Such a "demand" presumes a sort of human exceptionalism that I often find myself arguing against – as Clément quips, "Today, the ecological fortune of the planet depends on the human species and elections." This also presumes a form of inverted free will – a choice of what not to do, a choice to stand back, stand down, give way, make space for the more-than-human. A Dantean love such as we find in *Purgatorio* – a *terraphilia* that is the seed of "a common space of the future" (Clément), and which sweeps aside bad government (*mala condotta*) – these are the capacities we need to traverse the broken ground that lies ahead of us. Diaspora becomes a recalibrated *paradiso* only when we imagine the entire planet as a mobile garden – a *jardin en movement* – plants and people moving where they need to.

Detail from William Blake, *The Lawn with the Kings and Angels*, photo courtesy of the National Gallery of Victoria, Melbourne

SKETCH OF A POEM I WILL NOT HAVE WRITTEN:
A BLAZING SPACE

drowned in deluge or thirsty, burned, hopeless onslaught
no, modern life, i do not submit. no, climate disruption, i sing to rising Sun
i am Planting fields of baby Trees who will be thousands of years old.

—ANNIE ROSS

FIRST MOVEMENT

I tried to speak of the
times but there were
too many and
                        glancing
some like blows turned

in a twilight they had
created turned and I'm
sure like a bird or
something more seed-like so

/ *even the mighty river burned* /

and darting bent back
on their lines of flight
so that the yellow trees
were our fellow
                        travellers

and gave what they had to
spore or to flames we
took to be the earth's own
vascular system unlocked by the
hot wind was our breathing was
                                    common
as the dense mycelial air

Always now and never
too moth-in-a-piano to attract
the light that remains unmade
as apple or pear tree making
journeys of sweet light sound

plant / animal / mineral / us

"we" are now listening
           within the usurpation

for the tree forms
sun into leaves & its branches
& saps are solid & liquid
states of
           sun

as these trees that are
beat gold against sky
of this burnt autumn that
goes on glowing and glowing

Let us restore
chance to this
climate of determinacy
throw singed notes into
the wilderness the
                    future is
change I will say
not as vicissitude
or individual will
but as patterned
                    movement
all I desire is
patterned social movement
pulsing musically towards
what wilderness
                    the future is
blow-by-blow
the fire and the flood
inspiriting sentient trees
if this isn't a revolution
I won't even hum the tune

SECOND MOVEMENT

Where there's fire
there's water too
hillsides burnt in summer
slump inundated in winter
no trees to keep
no soil to hold
aspen bristlecone hemlock
pine spruce and ash
and ash and ash and
water roar
swept into ravine
into vortex into
fished from a sky of fire
rushed torrent to acidic sea

Words made
for singing and chanting
just silent here
no inert world
is not ours
is its own fire
built and banked
between verges
feels sorrows
exalted joys
though not by those names
elm alder poplar
maple and spruce
have their own
revolutions
their own red
which turns us back
and folds us in again
falling mountains
swollen rivers
a *pétroleuse* loose
in the heart of every crying bird

Sifting through
the creatureliness of it all
cold fire struck
in winter sky

dinosaur us
flat on the earth
looking ever upward
into our mingling despairs

Everything that changes quickly
is explained by fire
hearts skies and
the depths of mutable substance
this other I am

shines in paradise
burns in hell
in cookery as in apocalypse
our fate sealed
with Icarian wax

Last night talking
was more than "talking"
it was burning
words in each other's
thermal hearts

fire was the element
the sky called to
but only rain came
rain after rain and then
the fire remained in the cold sky alone

somewhere in a land
I'd like to be able to remember
every plum blossom
co-regulating
clings to the sound of bees

I started to feel
around this time
a woodenness within
new fire kindling
heat where only water
moved over soundless stone

The I consumes itself
yet I did not join the fray
the beloved world around me
burnt or was washed
from its perch in possibility
I did not move or weep

Sunken states are
sunk in the heart / knees buckle
in the climate of disaster
I am only broken to be
whole / only whole when
I am with others equally broken

I've held certain truths
to be self-evident

they weren't

my brothers burn
facts they forge
in caloric heat
everything aflame
oil fires piped to the feast
turn us on a spit of desire
all that is fuel is policed
all that is policed is
banked fire
all that we've unearthed
we / un-earth / ourselves

don't dream too much water
police will simply cross it too
give us just enough water
to wash away police forever
after the flood
and mutual light
give us glowing embers
placed against glowing embers
give us high ground and
safe harbour and
love and love and love

I fall back
fall and bend

back into the
little that is mine

small simultaneity
time and nowness

a line I take for free
from another writing

most of my organs
play in other churches

that are not churches
but pianos with moths

raising riot at sea
over volcanic aspirations

FIRE FIRE FIRE
Flood Flood Flood
bright blaze to the river
all trees and plants soon on fire

tamarisks willows elm trees
celandine rushes and galingale
        the garden moves
with wing and wind
        the shrapnel of life
escaping the wounds

its goal *to string*
pyrolytic moments together
for as long as possible
but the garden
                the garden

want to think "apple"
seed-planted brain
Arum palaestinum / black calla lily
Rubus ulmifolius sanctus / za'atar / zaytoun

we're not birds
writes Fady Joudah
but light

- 16 -

I write because
I can't sing
in thick dark
waking beyond matter
hearts and wind
depart for islands
no power
less unbearable
than love
the permanent eclipse
hell not the sole
            owner of fire
the middle of the street
not the only place *love*
                bursts
a bull whirling in the sky
the great dancer
suspended midst
three ghosts of poets I love
plum blossom clinging
to plum blossom
                        trembling

THIRD MOVEMENT

Not for want of trying
the sea boat and night of memory
without birds how are there havens
what urgency is there
what time for poems and movements
when all poems are cut from time's
stretched cloth / so *plunder, O poet*

words / seeds / let beauty keep me
off balance yet searching and trying
for the life of me to grow a goddamn
wing in the mind / oar in the earth
fir and birch and beech fly back
all the way back before the future
begins to burn everything again

Tree halo and
taste of spent volcano

every myrtle is
a tree long unknown to me

a mountain something
looming in dream

dark vertical smudge
at the back of time and sky

more bullet holes in this distressed world
than I've seen blown through

passing tanagers their
flight the tangerine of

smallest skies this side of
where the fires yet burn away hills

So if
in other temporal registers
all about movement
of so many synchronous birds
we had not to name
but release into eternities
of their own autonomous making

cf. nest architecture
bowl and basket form
.seeds in a dark cave of
rejectamenta
green, rose-red, lapis
a faint *track in the sand from*
a plum tree just now maybe to bloom

In the shock of the catastrophe
pools that circle counter-clockwise
at the banks of the river
bending time backwards
an infinite loop that actually leads
nowhere which is
likely what beauty is

and those
/ dormant volcanos all /
who produced the inferno
glide on as swans
whose busy feet we do not see
living remnant of *what words conceal*
these notes I leave you and yours etc.

How great a burden we
are for each other
between the "no longer and
not yet" – the deep gorge of
the human body possessed by those who feel
the catastrophe in their very bones

though the bone-frame held
the heart's dead ember / this elemental shame
that we are human and not feathered
and did this to the weathered world
where I hum bee sounds
                                    badly
just a barely remembered seed-song
of what once was called our common identity
the bridge … between invisibility and invisibility

This burrows into me
this tiny seed of time and
language / will out of willow
asp out of aspen moving
no revolution now until
catastrophe opens the door
recursive / input / loop

The fires consume the firs
possibly we will reach haven
diasporic torrent
of another voice I did not invent
but found by the side of a river
running wild through the bare trees
of a language I never knew how to speak

Since when could one only
be decent by welcoming death?

a burnt mountain asked a cloud
on its way to the river to the sea

the One who knows the secrets of the human heart
beside the *vast machines of administrative mass murder*

I study the grain, stains, and scratches on this desk
hand moves / is another / word temple / avian soul

unlike silkworms and butterflies
we do not leave the stage swiftly enough

but linger over the word "history"
which "we" craft in "our" uncommon image

instead / be the bird in the *flowering of the burnt wood*
seed cracked after fire / where we only expected ash and ash and ash

FOURTH MOVEMENT

Between the books
on the shelves
and the branching
of the mind
scale and relation
through wilderness
                          and pang
everyone with a language take
one step forward
and the entire forest takes
one step forward
and so *Macbeth* etc.
the raven upsetting
its cousins the crows
out damned spot
I love you too much
little cousin   little relation   out out
fold yourself back into the relentless dark
of the ache   of the ark

/

As above / so below
stars you cast magic across ceiling blue
or down into dark water's phosphorus glow
on *the burning beach*

the unimaginable turbulence of relation
because everything is alive
moving / shifting
feet on the ground
                          head in the sky

This consecrated branch transmits to posterity
the benefits of seeds or buds hidden in trees
                              for thousands of years

I see /
             burning mountains and valleys
rejuvenating fire passing through
then the waters beyond passed through too
slashed across with shafts of light

I think /
                  we might be on a purgatorial climb
through cleansing not infernal fire
towards the place free will and climate action
are supposed to meet
soluble tones sung from the forests within
and just outside the door
                              the whorls of time

Traveller /
                  what really are your reasons?
"We" broke the world and
"we" still don't know who or what "we" are
or that "we" are not separate from
rivers of persons
fire-flecked plants and animal havens
constellations burrowed into any night's sky

And so Brân sailed not through waters
but through an orchard long in bloom

treacherous growth
where no distributive justice shines

these sighs of spirits of those whose homes
were burnt or dashed by flood or bombardment

a journey through the otherworld
to marvellous isles and back

so that when they returned all the forests were gone
and stepping ashore they turned into piles of ash

as if they had been on earth for hundreds of years
I am in the middle, the middle, the me

a tree that's animate / an upright tower
made to bend by a river flowing far away

FIFTH MOVEMENT

In leaded blue windows
in blue frames and blue forms

the cinder cone trembles
the river runs coarse

I reassemble forest trees
I defenestrate cyan blues

there is fire in the west
there are mobile seeds on the wind

someone yell "timber"
someone leap from a towering tree

here comets put down dinosaurs
here comets put an end to markets

let me also be meteoric
let me also climb deeper into forest dark

Enigmas forever
to one another
hand in hand
on this green earth
not to surpass
planetary limits
but as collective
atlases or turtles
to heft aloft
this felt home
and carry us
starward
or stagger as
guardians of the
empty intersection
and the mysterious fact
that language can
even exist at all
or anything be named
tree mountain river
or universal healthcare

Bewildered hills and sky
of fire   or backlit
by burnt orange glow
or molten earth after
siphoning all the
water away / it is all
molten earth / everything
is or was alive
                    the trees will
yet lift up out of nowhere

what time is it now?
what Alps are calling us / Hölderlin
what rivers soothe?
                         years later
and long out of forests
the silence
of cities *keens*
                    walker
in these avenues
deafness is our only barricade

The country of poets
is being bombed again

see the clouds of word-dust
billowing into televised air

cries out of burnt nights
metred but tending towards

a fractured syntax
and the unexpected image

not a dove
but a singing mechanical bird

perched on a tank's gun
its new rhythms

the staccato of RPGs
the phosphorous of *idiot wind*

Just a little
zärtlichkeit
more than ever
what we need
this earth not
heavens streaming

resist states and
nations swallowing nations for
debts become us
go instead at plant pace
go circling commons bounds
and welcome new arrivals home

Vertiginous
forward sweep
noisy black-caps
golden-crowned sparrow
that words should
be like columns
temple or forest
in their roughness
and irregularity
the stone under
pinnings of
the sky of
stars and bombs
and the silences
between them
we long for
or fear

Out of the evidence of wreckage
out of the night
                    song
the convection wind and
the carbon war
in the middle of our quaternary crisis
leaking what water we have left
into the unquenchable desert
/ oil prices rise
                    states cool to change /
with only fragments to shore
neither beginnings nor endings
but always scarred *becomings*

Are you
still there
a lapis night
twisting
apple knees
starred with
empyreans
quietly sounding
through the trees
or am I only
just now beginning
to understand
the depths of
my longing
and how far it is
across the eras
to where you are
turning alone
in shade of
your orchard
dancing
the universe
back into
being

What madness knows
lies outside history
silence   welling up in song
my sky was iron   I was made of stone
but   *profoundly scathed*
drunk with light and the spirits of plants and *animals*
watching clouds move in the dark
the very ground burning with Greek fire
upright   only in cadence of grace or spin

Nightsong
I lend you the pen of birds
the arcs of their flights
maths or orbits
dim lights out of dark
that strike
in the very world
which is the world
of all of us

And the earth held itself
in good balance
which was no consolation
for those winging
into cold mountains
and tumbling waters
loaded with nightsongs
singing over roads
that are broken
burnt vehicles
the sound of a jet
a column of armaments
so long it rings the earth
and still never arrives
at its destination
hoping only
that we come back
as rain over wildfires
swept towards the coast

Nightsong
I am failing
in the simplest task
to lift another up
when again and again
all I can do is
lie down beside them
listing *all the ravages*
from which the earth proceeds

the seeds of strange apples
I have gathered
in my travels
and propagated
myself

The Mediterranean remains
the deadliest border in the world
the pull factors
vast inequalities and the lure
of a livable life
reeling in world-shudder
these battering years
now history
           now history

but this moment too
the violence of capital
the madness of growth
a shark turning to bite
at its own soft insides
        look at us groaning
fury
      in the abyss of climates

Poets
free as starlings
and just as devastating
in coordinated flight
the wicks of mountains lit
and the waxen world running down
words gather into instant
and fleeting pattern

I so long for the
Carpathians' coiled
and listening ear
and the breezes telling
all rivers which
way to run

Fearless tremble
what if you
walking out of
madness kept
a skylark locked
in your cage
rattling ribs?

You are walking
Bordeaux or other
wine-kempt region
with colossal
stride the Neckar
is an illusion of your
yellow home flooding

Sitting at the edge
of the forest
wrenched in dark
volcano economy
each animal home
a flood from rocks
above this liquid
earth pump hot then
washed down cold
as at borders the
rivers say you've
not swept us clean
for years   star-eyes
indeed we tried to
bomb their waters
but the wounds
closed over ordinance
and the currents
swift continued as
electric spirit's delight
thrown over fences
and those forests flames
grew red-hot shoots
towards mountains crashing
mountains' ash towards
the ground still trembling

And then this too
in riot of moments

on a burning path under pines
or in dark of sturdy oaks

lovers might yet
walk away from war

or right on through it
if these trees still matter

or if matter still has a hold
on shared human hearts

near rivers and under rain
of rockets

what name
should I give this stranger?

Make a boat
out of an apple tree
a star from
projector's light
sail into borderless
distance where futures
fruit if we are human
and animal
and plant
at once
ungainly and
if in there new
floating trees small birds
still sing and still have
wings to cross on
moth wing seed case and burr
fragrance of a thousand
peaks now *burst into flower*

We've only *served*
the sunlight lately
and present world events
glow as embers in the
smoke-filled air
or glitter beneath the
surface of fast-rising tides

mind from too much
literature unsound
notes in lexicons
and notes played
notorious on piano
moth-winged compulsions
to repeat certain words or notes

And if you are
still growing towards me
apple branch
and blackberry cane
I will wait like a wind
that keeps to the cliff edge
and waits for the trees'
boughs to reach out
and be clipped by my
patiently roiling currents

But the crater
my love
exerts its terrible pull
on one so dimmed
by desires they refuse to dispel
under a harmful compulsion
to wander into woods
where every bough leans towards you
my own way lightless
for I have put out all the lights myself

The usurpation grinds on
nations take other
nations as spoils
they were wrong to be
nations in the first place
rather than silt places
and swift glacial placings

and rivers swollen
from mountain fastness
while among the ruins
under apophenic light of stars
migrants hold council
with the plants and animals
they have saved from deportation

Singer of rivers reversing time
scarred whole to
burnt spun planet
this only not
trash but treasure
no climate for poets no
climate for least weasel or great blue heron

like a brook I am
carried away
by the expanding end of something
Asia or
an old dream of continents
asleep on their long journeys
over their deep magma beds

Remnant *selva antica*
forest of the mind
and the humus that grounds
the human
            shadows
that tell us
growth is suffering
we dwell in the disclosure
in the cutting and clearing
when will we turn our cities
into forests again
and climb towards new nests
and hollows
and listen to the subterranean
voices of the dead
we are always already
receding back into shade
of intimate animal being
leaping limb to limb
in post-glacial labyrinths

Somewhere between
stuff and structure
the boundless forest
grows in the night
they drop bombs amid
the swaying trees
to no effect
the green comes closer
the shadows extend over us
birds thread through
trunks and boughs

the only light filtered
through chlorophyllic green
I want you green
the only water filtered
through moss and mycelium
we've come this way before
but we got lost then too
selva oscura
nel mezzo
nel mezzo
the forests were always
asylum
refuge and haven
places of exile
of hiding and outlawry
the shelter
of the other
we yet long for
in poetry and life
in torrential times

They became
fleets of ships
cargo holds
containers
everything animal sent below
every plant flexible policed
(invasive / endemic)
bewildered wildernesses
tree-blind *terraphilia*
the world's scoured clean
crossing the boundary into

nonhuman depths
the practice of the forest
returns to practice us
wildflowers
resinous gold fields
taken under wings
and wings and wings

THE MIDDLE

THE MIDDLE

Do you know what limbo means?

—ABDULRAZAK GURNAH

And should a stranger come
Ashore from shipwreck,
Lamenting home or some
Lost friend ...

—FRIEDRICH HÖLDERLIN

CANTO 1

Boat of leaves
little ship
I'm yours
in dead air
of profound night
words
don't bind me
she who moves me
moves and directs
light in search
of freedom
where the wave beats
the sun just now rising
without a word
turned back
like one who found
the lost road again
upon the gentle grass
that never has seen
sail upon it

CANTO 2

People
emerging from
their journey
across the sea
for a moment
as wings
wanting no oar
nor sail between
eternal pinions

embrace me
here where I am
making this journey
even now as one who goes
without knowing the direction

/

The meridian stretches
people pondering
through thick vapour
a light across the sea
I didn't know what
took shape as wings
neither oar nor sail
more radiant
a vessel of such lightness
strangers
flung on the beach
harsh and
I was not one of them
always there

with my body
coming to this country
all the others
settled in a meadow
flew up at once
and fled the coast

CANTO 3

O clear and
open land
broken
spacious
body in which
I cast a shadow
to traverse the infinite
these people
let's go to them
still distant
light on the ground
and all the others
following closely
this is a human body
turn and look
surrendered
and weeping
close beside
the bridgehead
turned back
at the end

CANTO 4

Conscious of
the something
error holds
as I listened
in the hedge
the two of us
can climb to the
top pressed
on all sides
I made myself crawl
towards the sun
revolving closer
imagine a single horizon
then you will see
light
at the beginning
and a voice
from which I still have not
caught my breath
come now
climb ahead of me
see the meridian
touch the shore

CANTO 5

Climbing we saw
folk approaching
no place for the
sun's light to pass
shadow rend
the clear sky
in the same limbs
you were born in
blood enthralled
within my heart
I was overtaken
I fell
I staggered
turned back to
mist and wind
and the rain fell
and the earth rushed
to meet the river

/

Flushed
along the hillside
the rays of light

make it plain
at nightfall
poet

in those same limbs
until the last hour
cannot recognize

the footsteps
that land on
orizons

poured from a moment
that brings cares
took you far away

a stream
one little tear
that vapour gathers

turns into water
with intellect stirred
mists and great peaks

the rain fell
the gullies
tearing its way

my frozen body
the long journey
made then   unmade me

CANTO 6

And those
brutal
hands
on body
O light
she speaks to you
you will see her soon
for now I am not weary
the hillside is hidden
I keep on walking
ship without pilot
in the terrible storm
look in your heart
day and night call to you
preparing tyrants
the subtle threads
they spin
currencies   laws
no comfort no bed
in *mezzo novembre*

CANTO 7

Said again
the fault
was not something
revealed

the ground saying
only night's darkness
will lead us
to that place

make our way
serene translucent amber
the wounds
where the water's born

where the indigo wood
the grass and
the fragrance of
a thousand scents

branches
from kingdoms
singing

CANTO 8

Look there!
the celestial hawks
melt the sea
a bell ringing
as though sweetly
longing remembers
pierced with
flaming swords
in newborn leaves
my gaze blurred
how long is it since
the sorrowful region
of my first life?
and I am still
sitting here pleading
with the stars
no ramparts
wheel round your will
misguiding the world
fixed firmly
in the middle

CANTO 9

Gleaming in the
shape of animal
and memory captive
to sorrowful song
far from and
less close to
our thinking wings
outspread terrible as
lightning / both caught
fire in that
imagined blaze in
her arms and
I became no
colour / that walls
slept within you
let me take
this one up
who lies asleep
and set out
on what seemed
white marble some
rough stone a
singed arid rock
porphyry flaming red
on the threshold
time opening and
locking at once

CANTO 10

Turning one side
to the other
I would be
put to shame
for many years
had passed
in the same way
caught up
in gold
as a person
eager for any new thing
I cannot
untangle what is coming
unknot in vision
the sickness
when we are
as it were
imperfect insects
upon our backs

CANTO 11

The green endures
wind comes
and goes
my heart
remains
confined by bounds
ourselves
have suffered
ourselves
burdens
what can be said
made clean and light
move your wings
bear this weight
brightly
when old
resound
to the very edge of life

CANTO 12

I went on
like one who
has to follow
memory's creatures
crushed by the
gigantic project
glum upon the shreds
of cavernous ruin
don't look down!
with sail and oar
memory sculpts
any creature
looking bewildered
in the road
the mountain
sun's course
time clothed in
white said come
with wings struck
I seemed
much lighter almost
I don't know what
this learning
incised upon me

CANTO 13

In front of us
the bare road
the centre of
motion
unless some
other speaks
the earth
would not have
what they need
words the only
place I stitch
them up
sure of seeing
farther ahead
I mend my harm
I was mad
I believed
I had free eyes
and land
to long for

/

As it turns
the hinge of movement
some other spoke
and went on
out of hearing
as if each
endured in their voice
through the future
any mind's true city

I call myself
enemy of the state
I think
the torment
will not be long
already we
hear the earth
returning

CANTO 14

Journeying from
[hide the name]
I do not know
from out the ocean
from some valley
like cattle
leaving so that
a thousand years
fill with trouble
from mountain to the sun
when I remember
their names
full of weeds
the house
and love
and the footsteps
of the rest of your family
[never will be safe]
walk away
say nothing
draw closer
to the earth
silence
gives comfort

CANTO 15

That sphere
plummeting
a sort of parasol
I thought
as we walked
if there is company
each becomes richer in it
the more there are
the more love
you will deliver
at once
out of sorrow
waters running down
towards the earth
things are real
someone
eyes glazed
tripping
will tell you
do not refuse
to open your heart
to the abounding waters
pouring towards nowhere

CANTO 16

Beneath
a vacant sky
smoke
as if still
not loosened
tell me tell me
I knew the world
what you ask me
I may see
their motion only
all of them
although free
are subject
entangled
modernity a veil
over word and measure
unfasten my way
tell me tell me
what I loved
confounding
bad governments
Gaia already
growing brighter

CANTO 17

The mountains
couldn't see
the sun
things outside us
that bird's singing
the water
veils its image
let us try to go
a wing
restored
but without love
well-being
cannot be conceived
neighbour
pushing down neighbour
I would have the mind
caught in cloud
begin to disperse
the outer world
moves
the bird that sings
now you have lost me!
though broken
light struck my face
a voice said
Here is the ascent
those sovereign words
turned like a boat
the heart
sundered and standing
against reason
acquiring seed

/

Give me
the possibility of song
without words
to dissemble it
just that
timeless movement
that mezzo
that seed
lodged deep in
wood of each
heart
sewn symphonic
as *uccelli* soar
the only terminus
a *carmen perpetuum*
of walled-around world
or wing
or sail
or feeling stream
touched by pilgrims
that keep
coming ashore

/

Remember
if in mountains
caught
thick heavy vapours
measuring your steps
out of clouds
the dying rays
on the shore

moving light
and the lazy oar
digging in again
and the bird
that delights
the mind
like a bubble
now you have lost me!

Then a voice said
here is the way up
new light struck
my imagination
quickening desire
let's go
before it's dark
so spoke my guide
and I with him
turned our steps
and felt a wing brush
and paused there as a ship
run up on a steep beach
that no creature
ever was without love
that seeds in you
and can never turn against
and cannot be divided
itself from the other
that is root and fruit of
everything moving in step

CANTO 18

Drawn by
everything
love is born
in movement
all nature
in motion
understanding
in the bee
such urgency
is primal
a power in you
kindled by
a burnished path
the sun inflames
others cannot
weep remembering
body ran
so swiftly ahead
that in my mind
I rambled to and fro

CANTO 19

Crooked life
in cold limbs
on the sea
eyes singing
open circles
thought making
earth split
mantle opens
without looking
we outstretched
our weeping
mid-ocean
the earth
herself cleaves
the imagination
that creature
without which
there is no order

CANTO 20

The vacant spaces
that fill the world
with animal poverty
attention changes
when we perceive
humble life
tell me if I finish
the journey
according to the feeling
that drives us on our way
insatiable sweet fury
the whole kingdom
a hidden line
as long as daylight lasts
I seem alone
the distance shudders
so came and stood
beside her
like first hearers
desirous of sound
hurrying along the roadway

CANTO 21

By that water
lying at our feet
we turned
in everlasting exile
only now felt
greater when the
thirst is greatest
your own words
summoned me
from the flame
tangled in poetry
that each springs
from a gesture
one silent
the other
afraid to speak
but I would have you
be sure
the love for you
that burns in me
makes me forget emptiness

CANTO 22

Kindled
by other passages
one can feel
disproportion
spread its wings
the springing waters
of Parnassus
my poem
holding the lantern
as we took our way
how often we remember
intensity
left behind
by a tree
by the road
high rock
clear water
and a voice
and completeness
and we were nourished
and content

CANTO 23

Come
approach
a crowd
their faces
withered to a crust
the people who
could make that happen
what made them?
do not ask me to speak
of excess
the tops of the green leaves
you exchanged the world
for future time
swift-preparing sorrow
not only I
but all these
with me
through the deep night
climbing and turning
around the slopes

/

Time
sung and wept
silent and unknown
a husk
who could believe
the cause
do not make me speak
a power is in that water

a measure we sense
moved
I thought I saw
a future
quick-moving
around me
and I am shook
all these folk too
shook

CANTO 24

We pressed on
with hollow eyes
saying tell me whether
I am beautiful or good

none spoke
that I could hear
love dictates
my pen to follow

I felt the wound
of new poetry
form between styles
every day more pillaged

in this realm
I lose too much
remain behind
with the poets
shouting into the foliage
in a drunken state

dejected
we went on
saw glass or metal
in a furnace

the breeze of May
bringing fragrances
and felt soft feathers
brush my brow

CANTO 25

Without stopping
one after the other
lit out
for all haste
you move
your image moves

words remain human
like blood coagulates
and quickens
like a plant
or sea fungus forming
from the begetter's heart

once articulate
such art of nature
how the sun's heat
turns into wine
breathing
memory and will
radiate many colours

follow the fire
wherever it may go
for every sense moves us
within the great burning

so that I looked at them
and spoke to the forest
faithful to the woods
all things through time burning

CANTO 26

Not because of
slowness
but for a wall
against people
some towards Libya
some escaping and
all lamenting
their astonishment
so I was moved
to know each by name
the fool's concern
for truth
to be granted access
as much as we in
this world need
so he disappeared into
the flames he'd pointed to

/

If my attention
turns
the whole
deep red
could answer
to the sun
to kiss each
before they take
the first step
towards the desert
fleeing they return
free to come with us

themselves the
human law
whoever has come
a long way
to harbour
through the fire
words peerless
in all of them
free to walk
in this world
through the fire
amazed
open-mouthed
and whole

CANTO 27

When I
imagined a full
thousand years
vexed
into boiling a
light there the
disappearance
of my shadow
nature took
the tops of the hills
but in that little space
I saw stars
before dawn
whose rising
is to pilgrims
a gift and art

/

So fading
a voice
full of fire
I became
the fire
speaking
within
come this way!
into the flames
and begged Statius
to follow
in boiling glass
walked on and

sang light
speed your steps
cut countries into
a single realm
for nature now
broke up
on the crags
and all night long
I could see the stars
asleep in a meadow
ever the traveller
I rose and found
so many branches
that at each step
I felt the gift
of grass and trees

CANTO 28

The forest
wandered
slowly
the small humming
pine wood
bending time
and keeping waves
under eyelids
surging light
love I said
there are things
to change and
conflict and struggle
its own cause
utterly free
in the living air
plants' movements
full of seed and
will and words
so that I turned
to my poets and
saw if they had
been listening or if
memory is always spring

CANTO 29

The forest
kept pace
in that bright air
blazed up
like new-kindled fire
flames moving towards us
only the river
kept me from them
I could see
new-sprung grasses
full of eyes
their forms
golden birds' wings
the emerald earth
sharp and brilliant
those glimpsed from afar
coming once more
to fill the space
between us when
the lady turned towards me

/

Saying the last word
she raced through
the great forest
shining brighter and brighter
like a fire blazing
brighter than the moon
moving in our direction
an illusion like
a mirror showed me

the air painted
in all colours
and my mind
opposite me seemed
four animals
eyes full of feathers
for I am pressed
out of cold places
all wings and bird parts
Africanus
I saw the earth
burnt up and red
I could have tasted
these pleasures
I saw a sword
shining in the distance
a sound of thunder
and that noble company
seemed forbidden to go any further

CANTO 30

Voice
scattered
stars
rising or setting
had not a lady
left at the sound
of my name
do not weep
the festival
went on like
someone speaking
but seeing myself
I drew its shadow
around it singing
turned breath to water
for rain is new life
my second age changed
my beauty become false
the more rank and
tangled grows the land

/

Speaking as
a person removed
from the land
of those who turn
water into anguish
each seed
raining down
seemed the gift
of weeds

the earth become
new life
imploring the water
freely crossed
with my tears
on other ships it was
sweetest dew

CANTO 31

Speak
say whether
that voice
forced out of
love leading
to abandon the shame
of my mistakes
the limbs
of my dying
uprooted by the storm
bird's nests and arrows
returned to the ground
the cord and the bow
a dance made by
light shining on water
those radiant eyes
primal creatures turned
towards what I became
pulled me down
into the world
that thing that in itself
remained unchanging
animal shadowed
only by the loving sky

CANTO 32

Crossing
I followed

through the distance
the tree rose

in its own colour
I would depict how I passed

into splendour
render the word compassionate

to which she answered
fix your eyes

on those lights
in their hands

a dense cloud coming
and a vessel fleeing

O my little boat
heavy with grief

covered by wild grass
through the forest dragged

CANTO 33

If I speak to you
brother
why do you not listen?

she rose and stood upright
my dearest sister
she then said / brother

disengage from
fear and shame
as stars or feathers

entangle yourself
in constellations
be not mended

already it is harder
to solve this enigma
a singular water with a stony hue

the tree petrified
in written form
and stamped into you

see whether it
can follow the earth
made a stranger

remember your failure
go as naked as the sun
teach longing

forgetfulness
rising from the Tigris
and Euphrates

the Alps flowing
from the single river
of another's will

and the loom of this canticle
remade the way trees are new
when their leaves also are new

GARDENS IN MOTION

If we take the Italian word for paradise – paradiso – and rearrange the letters, we get diaspora *... A whole new exercise could be inherent in this anagram, one that might slowly shift the address of paradise.*

—INGER CHRISTENSEN

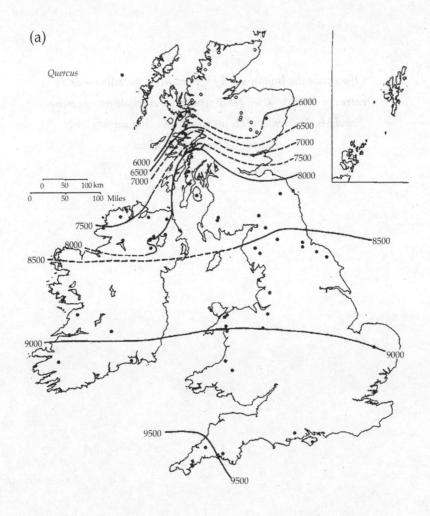

Map charting the recolonization of Britain by Quercus (the oak) after the end of the Last Glacial Maximum, from Figure 25.1, Examples of historical and contemporary range dynamics, Jean François Le Galliard, Manuel Massot, and Jean Clobert, "Dispersal and Range Dynamics in Changing Climates: A Review," *Dispersal Ecology and Evolution*, ed. Jean Clobert et al. (Oxford University Press, 2012) reproduced with permission of the Licensor through PLSclear

GARDENS IN MOTION

Went out to walk at plant pace
long arcing stride of *Rubus* stepping canes
coastal rainforest zone Pacific mists
to berry and behold
if we ever come this way again the seeds were saying
sown on the wind and trampled on the trail
gut-carried and shat forward
mycelium inching beneath the forest's shifting fringe
some forgotten corner of the holy forest
bees' jet-black bodies and blue iridescent wings
time-lapse and our lapse in timing
no future as sure as less-abundant being
peeps over horizon and squints at liquids lost
the sheer level of paralysis etc. etc.

/

How the fretful world turned wanderer
changed by deep sky rivers
and aching animal movements

sad music and aching joys
the motion of all things
therefore let us walk dear sister

let the mountains be free and
a dwelling place for sounds of woods
and lofty cliffs and shooting lights

and guide the language
of wild minds
tender voice I can hear no more

/

Moving northwestward in search of moisture
wood density and seed weight
spatial shift of species abundance

cheat grass tansy blackberry thyme
fifteen to twenty kilometres per decade
median poleward and upland shift

more sensitive to moisture than temperature
association between seed size and
directional movement / wind vs. animal pollination

repeated plot-level measures
infiltrating by creep of root and shower of seed
a landscape we have made impassable

necessitating long-distance leaps
dispersed outlier populations
refugia serving as loci for more rapid invasion

/

The distance a propagule falls
seed wings of plumes
if vigorous uplift lofts

long-distance bird agents
or nuts cached along forest edges
human agency as super disperser

profoundly altering disturbance regimes
habitat fragmentation stranding plants
without egress from remnant sites

decreased bird populations
decreasing plant dispersal
let alone the godforsaken bees

take silent advantage of human mobility
ride shotgun on quests and catastrophes
riparian and littoral variations bloom

montane landscapes may shelter
strong correlation between topographic slope
and horizontal velocity of temperature change

the grain of analysis and
the size of the kernels used to calculate
spatial and temporal gradients

we make no assumptions about
the tolerances of individual species
or migration speeds required to avoid extinction

plants are just slow animals
moving with purpose
sensing varying conditions

and generally knowing
where their bodies are in space
so we are more plantlike than

we would like to think
though without contraries
there is no progression

/

Arranged together in new combinations
mobile beings heading back and forth
new ecosystems replace old

often after fire or flood
people remain the strongest driver
rearrange the plant world to serve their needs

seeds and spores
little genetic fingers that will
grab hold wherever they are able

resilient sugar maple tracking the climate
but what is a Sequoia National Park without sequoias
Joshua Tree National Park without Joshua trees?

the question whether they can reach new ranges
species leaving and new species arriving
though death is a part of that story too

when the old plants die
the tension is released
new species flood in

fire the especially visible
catalyst of change
long heat waves insect blooms

last time the earth cooked
after 200,000 years the plants came back
long voyagers in search of a place to begin again

but what was it like in the middle?
turfed us out and settled to windward
I've got a bundle of sticks to proffer

don't worry we are getting to the story
jittered animal body mass
the lack of a shared phylogenetic history

and the epic song of
isoclines and climate velocity
the sweep of easy wind and downy seed

/

Mailed north in mobile climate envelopes
small steps along a front or
long-distance jumps

species with longer generations move at slower rates
seed shadows billowing
carried to high altitudes by updraft vectors

or however many kilometres before the
seed-eating creature shits the new mobile
plant colony forward

seeds with hooks or barbs
may take extended journeys
both surface and air vehicles can be chosen

even small seeds in the mud between toes
can be explorers of entirely new domains
bark-boring beetles

have arrived in the wood of transport palettes
taking the vectors of capital into their
invasion biology opportunism

time and space scaling
dynamic nesting of models
coarse to finer grids measured

lodgepole pine moving north facilitated by fire
and intrepid seeds riding rivers
to new alluvial and riparian dreamlands

Rubus a diasporic genus so widely spread
its small seeds easily tucked
in shirt pockets and bird crops

to climb into most climes as the word
scatter of fir out of fire and low
out of willow and pen out of aspen

written borders have no meanings
in undocumented third landscapes
middle of spacetime / middle of seedscatter

the shafts of time's light on bird wing falling
on *Rubus sanctus* / the Palestinian blackberry
the original burning bush lighting the way

/

I'm coming to the point
found a sprouting chestnut and planted it
now shading the door where I write

the tree asks what poetry is
arboreal and moving very slow
maybe it is a disordered devotion

or a baroque pattern
or *chaos-monde*
always in the middle of things

a balancing act of rhyme and ruin
though even chaos is not chaotic
poetry in motion / stays in motion

still I am confused too
planetary chaos is not fun to dwell in
all my plants are up and leaving me in the middle

my friends too are plant-like beings
throwing themselves forward to seed
in new times and places / sweet vernal times perhaps

curious I take down from the shelf Paul Friedrich's
Proto-Indo-European Trees:
The Arboreal System of a Prehistoric People

maybe I am hindcasting
maybe the pulse of our movements
is etymological and seeded in love long ago

I would speak in tree tongues
trace with rooting vagabonds the contours
of the newly reseeding garden in motion

PROTO-INDO-EUROPEAN TREES

We surmise
    the existence
        of ancestor languages

    and ancestor trees
their general vocalic nucleus
        a liquid

        the more exact
    shape of which
is not specified

the tree names
their meanings
    and botanical realities

        theories of nominal root structure
oak beams and
        paleobotanical pollen diagrams

e.g., where pastoralists
    cropped elm and linden shoots
        shouting names into the Arboreal Real

    that language and habitat co-hear
the dirt clinging to these phones
    and the fracas of migration patterns

/

Morphemes as clear-cut as trees
the parts of a chariot or
a tree are related anatomically

laks – lox – salmon – one of the oldest words
still held in our mouths
tasting sea and river in their bodies

feeding the roots of trees
we continually try to name
you apple maple elm and nut

a sort of verbal penumbra
the linden a precarious hypothesis
rivers of light veining canopy shyness

ash spear bone hafted
hornbeam household hewing
elm or linden with stone

subsystems of sound
covariational whether a morpheme
refers to juniper or cedar

paleobotanical tree inventory
fossil pollen from virgin forests
meadow groves and wooded riversides

genera evident in pollen
showing up in linguistic inventory
place and name honing each other

pollen inferred tree migrants
and PIE names accompanying each other
east and west over space and time

successional changes in relation to
climate and soil and the
contingent dependencies of biota

after fires and floods
pioneer genera emerge from
catastrophe speaking new diasporic languages

measuring the distance
from tree refugia
juniper after glacial retreat

then aspen and willow
then birch and pine
dominating the Preboreal

hazel with the Boreal
apple and maple in her tow
seeking the word "deciduous"

to speak oak and elm
and possibly frost-sensitive ash
a dramatic rise in response to climate change

accompanied by linden and
forming climax forests from Germany
to the Caucasus then

in the late Atlantic
hornbeam and spruce and fir
and the language that they used

such was the arboreal orientation
the oak becoming pervasive as
ayg- or *perk-* or *dorw-*

the Subboreal then marking
another abrupt climate change
winters growing colder

the beech spreading south and west
along with the Indo-Europeans
the walnut entered or was carried

/

Sound etymologies
echoing time's treeward movements
and findings across at least six stocks

all these meanings of *birch*
aspirated and medial liquid stops
to shine shimmer and gleam

to lighten whiten and be bright
to glitter flash blaze and glow
the shift to *ash* in Latin

thought to be motivated
by the absence of birch in these climes
(except in some highland niches)

covariation between names
and the ecology of tribes
brings us to the "beech-line" argument

which falls apart because of its
shifting habitat – extending south during
the Subboreal and flourishing far north

during the warmth of the Atlantic
likely present in Scandinavia
and Eurasian steppe before "hazel-time"

cold-hardy *Betula* came in early
dominating before the pine and hazel
producing enormous numbers

of minute two-winged nutlets which
after lying at winter temperatures
will germinate in the melting snows of spring

/

Cross-referencing the conifers
tar pitch and resin
a pattern which goes back to remote time

connoting – what? – differences
in the environments into which the speakers
of the daughterstocks moved?

You cannot derive a tree from a verbal root
say the parakeets in London planes
chipping sharp sound from shrapnel sky

Judging from the absence of its pollen
the fir was lacking in the fourth millennium
no one knew its name

fir species are geographically minded
the wind-resistant *Nordmannia*
and the temperate, hilly *Alba* hungry

for moist soils without late springs or early autumn frosts
the noble fir flourished with the beech
during the Subboreal, finding its tongue after dispersal

the spruce it's said grew on the edges of the language
known only to some of the speech community
running through the forest–steppe boundary

until mingling with and eventually yielding
to the Siberian spruce scattering its music across central Russia
and attaining its greatest growths in the Carpathians

climatic factors such as increased precipitation
helped spread the tree during the middle and late
Atlantic, though no pollen has been found in Ukraine

withdrew in the greater aridity of the Subboreal
speaking no tongues we can today reconstruct
silenced by the grey rain of the promiscuous *Pinus*

individual dialects developed fir terms
after their westward expansion
pine words seeming to cover most conifers at first

liquid and anomalous semantic grounds
also denoted rowboat or canoe / oar or even rudder
presumably oscillating for a time between juniper and cedar

cf. Homer's alder and poplar and fir
reaching to the skies long dry and well-seasoned
which would float for him lightly

both trees entered not long after the glaciers
with scale-like leaves silver-grey to cadet-blue berries
reddish shreddy bark and medicinal qualities

aspen or poplar we are trembling
from *osp through *aespe* and *wosa* and *opsa
to *wesp-* and *wopsa* (wasps) then through the weaving

to *wobhsā* (aspen's wings trembling) and so to the Latin
vespa (wasp) the spirant and stop in the tree word
an a-real term shared by the moistures

I would disambiguate the initial vocalism
useless as an oar or rudder on dry land
or the oar-shovel-scapula concatenation of *sphyá*

the trees shivering long into dispersal
an aspen stake driven into the ground of the grave
to prevent the corpse from leaving its coffin

a pioneer in geological succession
coexisting for some time with the willow
before being crowded out by the birch–pine complex

the Old Irish *sail* and Middle Welsh *helygen*
weep over lakes and rivers
Helicon no spiralling helix but a willow hill fluorescing

the achieving of which involved rough breathing
and views of meadows and other wet places
long lost to us now amid great dryings

the first willow word the verbal root of wind
turn twist and woven object
the exact form of which cannot be recaptured

so many of the speakers resident
along or near the great rivers
all favoured habitats of the moisture-loving tree

I assume that varieties of wild apple
diffused over much of Eurasia
between the Preboreal and the early Atlantic

try to resist the joke about apple PIE
the paleobotanical sources swooning
banishing hunger without sauce or ceremony

northern analogue of the grape
sweetness of life and circular celestial bodies
Virgil's *maliferae ... moenia Abellae*

vestige of the early intrusion of apple cultivation
the *B*s that do occur explained by borrowing
cheeks and knees and other beautiful parts of the body

honey or must apple laryngeal transitions
before the separation of the Anatolians
the liquids are almost identical

sweet life / sweet sweet life
beauty milked pressed and savoured
from minority members of the mixed hardwood forests

minimal radical elements – foods tools and religions
trees as living collaborators – in Latin *materia* means wood
what we've built we've built on wooden joists

I'd cart it all off as a measure
find the places trees used to sway and listen to the wind
soughing time and movement in their invisible branches

WALES VISITATION

these ancestors came over on ships made of trees from their lands
i doubt anyone asked these trees what they thought of this
or if they wanted to leave
knowledge keepers here say that trees communicate
from coast to coast through their roots
do you think some european trees miss their relatives?

—EMILY RIDDLE

IT WAS EARLY MAY when four of us
drove from the Midlands into northern Wales
on our way to climb Yr Wyddfa (Mount Snowdon).

Passing through Shropshire and
constantly navigating roundabouts
skirting tiny villages of grey stone and slate

I watched an aquamarine world unreel
sheep-dotted pastures dark woods rivers even the lowering sky
and fields appeared to be of related subaqueous shades of green

and as we sped on into the ancient Kingdom of Gwynedd
J explained the genre of electronic music known as "glitch"
which is said to adhere to an aesthetic of failure.

As digital technology began to allow the splicing together
of various small cuts and samples from previous recordings
the clicks scratches and other extraneous noises

produced in the process which would normally
be digitally smoothed out and covered over
began to interest some composers

who gathered the mistakes and editorial markers
slowed them down or stretched them out
and began to use them as percussive beats.

I stared out into an endless valley we sped along
with little on the hillsides to right and left
but crooked bushes ferns and rusty-hued vegetation

and then as the road wound higher only grey rock
and drifting mist / at Druid we turned off the main road
and coasted down into Bala.

Of Llyn Tegid Jan Morris says not even Lake Garda
is livelier than these waters on a bright summer afternoon
though it was not particularly lively this overcast day in May.

We walked along its meadowed frontage
then back through the town's narrow streets
until we stumbled upon the Norman ruin of the Tomen y Bala

the former keep now a grassy mound
the size of a large house with shrubs on its slopes
and crowned with a single willow we called *helygen*.

A sign near the entrance featured a close-up photograph
of two intense eyes and a deeply furrowed brow like the fixed
inquiring gaze found in certain painters and philosophers

who attempt to penetrate the darkness around us /
we piled back into the car and soon drove past the reservoir
that now covered the sunken village of Capel Celyn.

There is a persistent theme of inundation in Welsh tales:
glittering cities that lie beneath still waters
bells heard from the haunting deep and towers glimpsed

by fishers far down in the depths. One story
involves a minstrel performing at a feast in a magnificent palace
who begins to hear a voice urging departure

so she leaves climbs a hill above the palace and sleeps
beneath a hedge. When she awakes the waters of the mountains
have burst their bounds and the palace is now covered by Llyn Tegid.

We carried on the terrain changing often
the only constant being the ever-present threat
of a storm and the generally corrugated landscape

of desolate ridges hills valleys and mountains
a gap in banked clouds towering high in the west
occasionally allowing the rays of the sun to cast

a narrow beam down into the seemingly uninhabited depths
where the treeless substance of everything
appeared to be largely bare rock.

When we at last arrived at our lodgings in Aberdesach
we immediately walked down the lane to the sea
and out onto the shingle beach where a small river

snaked across the pebbled sands a calm finally coming over the coast
the clouds moving in gorgeously layered and mobile patterns
changing colour as the sun went lower and lower over the Irish Sea.

We took pictures and looked for the more interesting stones
before sitting on a low wall
like silent migrants having just stolen across a dangerous sea

unsteadily eyeing a new life on unrecognized shores
bereft of the trees plants and animals
that had been our companions in other climes.

/

THE WIND RATTLED the windows
and as the rains fell against them in frequent squalls
P read from a forestry report he found among the few books

stashed on a shelf beside old VHS tapes
and ugly figurines of druids prancing fiddlers
grimacing changelings and forlorn lake maidens.

Primeval Wales like much of western Europe
would have been covered by thick and diverse
broadleaf forests when human beings migrated into it.

As the last glaciers receded leaving behind a barren land
scraped clean by ice some juniper and pine
would have migrated across Doggerland first

and then alder and willow and birch and rowan
and holly and hazel and yew and beech and ash and especially oak
(*Quercus*) filled in the fresh land soon to become an island once again.

A tree is always an inscrutable traveller
only some three dozen tree species managed to cross
before Doggerland was inundated by the rising seas.

The ancient post-glacial forests only began to be cleared
with the arrival of Neolithic farmers
some six thousand years ago

so that just as the woods had once colonized the earth
so evermore-extensive fields of ash and cinders
now ate their way into that green-leafed world

sphagnum moss growth and bog development
followed the burning of native woodland in many lowlands
by the Bronze Age perhaps half of Britain's original forests were gone

and this process only continued with enclosure and the
British navy more or less finishing them off
and then marching inexorably / the armies of the conifer-forest plantations

transforming the look of Wales in half a century (Morris writes)
like invaders of some alien sensibility planted in stern disciplined ranks
the very opposite of the wrinkled coppices of oaks

whose place they have usurped. Today
woodland covers 15 percent of the Welsh landscape
and of that only a third is comprised of native broadleaf species

the rest are monocultural plantation conifers
the most common imported species being Sitka spruce
the most widely planted forest tree in Britain.

Wales was the folk memory of Europe (as Morris put it)
or its arboreal memory / it was an enormously ancient land
the detritus of the ages scattered all around its rough folds

it was also England's first colony
and I was born an uninvited guest in what was among its last
a west beyond the west / source of the spruce trees

that themselves had been transplanted back to this otherworld
and I thought then of a revolt the form of which human beings
had never yet imagined / a revolt that I expected or perhaps

merely wished for: molecular uprisings
symbionts turned parasites within their unwitting hosts
the tingling fungal nerve network of forests sending

the signal for the army of ancient trees to sweep downslope
and push us all at last into the rising sea
ready to reduce us to mere calcium and carbon waste.

It was then K read us the story of Brân the Blessed:
mortally wounded in Ireland the Welsh king of all Britain
ordered his seven companions to cut off his head

and return home with it. They obeyed and their journey
with the still-articulate head was long and winding
serenaded by magic bards and entertained by their king's head

at a feast that lasted not less than seven years
lodged in an enchanted castle with doors that must not be opened
and they are called the Assembly of the Wondrous Head

and travel in joy singing drinking and reciting ancient poems
until they happen to open a door they must not
and suddenly every loss they have ever suffered comes back to them

every kinperson missed / every failure of nerve or goodness or generosity
every ill that has befallen them / every injury received or given
every casual destruction of some small and incidental beauty of nature

every creature mistreated / every future possibility ignored
every weather pattern changed / every climate altered
every border imposed and defended against life's greater mobility.

/

I HAVE DRAWN the same tree every year for over a decade
an ancient and vast Sitka spruce which stands
tall and ragged over a beach on the Pacific coast of Vancouver Island

no trees the same size are anywhere nearby
it thrusts up from a sea of salal overlooking the massive beach
fronting the open ocean / mosses clump thick near its crown

and old broken and dead boughs clutched to its long trunk
like palsied or withered arms dangle below the still-green boughs above
its crown is flattened its canopy jutting and gnarled

bent and deformed / it is I think an ideally asymmetrical tree
from a species often known for their fearful symmetry
it would appear to care little for gravity

its wide base roots into the dense understory
on a steep slope where the path to the beach cuts beneath
its trunk is so straight and silver I think it is a main column of the heavens

it is at an evolutionary peak / a life form more durable and grand
and majestic than almost any other on earth
so that if visitors from another planet arrived

they would come first to this tree for greeting and instruction
bearing their gifts. What is your purpose?
To hold high in the sky for centuries a glowing habitat and beacon

for countless others to move towards / such thoughts seem inevitable
when I contemplate this giant tree whose company
is more and more the reason I yearn to return there each year

this is the place I empty myself find I am full only of wind and sea
salt vastness sound air tree mist made minor again by space and time
I spend my moments with particular stumps and trees

certain patches of sky framed a specific way
by spruce bough and salal spray. Unrecorded transactions occur.
It fills me with a feeling I cannot really describe. I suppose it is awe.

It stands where it always has seeming never to have taken a single step
holding up all the damage it has suffered twisted torn broken and scarred
battered by centuries of storm host to uncounted symbionts

parasites and hangers-on yet it stands calm and serene
feeling no urgency sending its seedlings forward confident of the centuries ahead
or at least fatalistically open to whatever its extended old age will bring

the world is gathered up in its boughs and will last as long as this tree lasts
I could not say how we were related but I imagined we are
or at least have some responsibility

towards one another / mine alone of which I could speak
being simply to remain there at the tree's side
as often as I could for as long as I could

being a minor supporting presence keeping silent company
and bearing witness to what we each differently knew of time
and the complex interweaving of life and death.

When I awoke in the morning
in the cottage near the beach at Aberdesach
it was with this tree having spread its roots and branches through my sleep

this dreamt conifer in this near-treeless world
living nest of all our natures
ship's mast of a landlocked vessel.

The Sitka spruce / *Picea sitchensis* / grows in a strip
of mist-shrouded maritime temperate rainforest
that lines the Pacific coast in a thin band northern California to Alaska.

German naturalist Georg Wilhelm Steller
accompanying Vitus Bering's Russian expedition in 1741
named the tree "spruce" deriving the name from "Prussian"

"Sitka" comes from the name of a Tlingit island and village / Sheet'ká /
typically taking a broad conical shape its branches grow
from regular whorls around the trunk

the needles bright blue-green on their upturned sides
whitish-blue with glaucous sheen beneath
they are pointed and prickly to careful touch

and grow in two rows shooting flat
bark flakes with age into purple or silver-brown plates
lifting their roundish edges to render the trunk rough

the lower trunk of the mature tree is free of branches
and the base often spreads into huge buttresses
individuals can live in excess of eight hundred years

and have been known to grow to astounding heights
epiphytes – smaller plants using the tree as their base
often grow on the trunk and branches

mosses lichens liverworts ferns and salal skirmish into bush
large shallow root plates host some hundred species of mycorrhizae
whose fungal networks form symbiotic relationships.

The nutrients of decaying salmon along river banks are also
important collaborators as are the bears that come for the salmon
and shit among the trees where salmonberries thrive.

Over millions of years newly evolved conifer species
including spruce began to spread south from higher latitudes
periodic cooling and warming shrinking or extending their ranges

like a pulse but generally they thrived near the damp Pacific Coast.
These trees rode out the Last Glacial Maximum
in small ice-free refugia between the tongues of advancing ice sheets

on the western edges of Vancouver Island and Haida Gwaii
where early human migrants to Turtle Island might have found themselves
in spruce-forest refugia / as the ice receded trees humans

and other species expanded their ranges concurrently
they built their ecosystems together as intimate companions
the roots leaves stems bark fibres and fruits of trees all have their human uses.

But I digress. What falls from the tree renews itself in the guise of poetry.
In the morning we woke early ready for Yr Wyddfa
packed quickly and soon our car sailed up through Caernarfon and then inland

like a spruce seed alight on its single wing
the night still heavy in my limbs
early sun casting long shadows as we came into a deep river valley

and the bounds of the valley were forest
and on either side of the river-level meadows
and on one side we could see a flock of white sheep

and on the other side we could see a flock of black sheep
and as one of the white sheep bleated
one of the black sheep would come across and would be white

and as one of the black sheep bleated
one of the white sheep would come across and would be black
and we could see a tall tree on the river bank

and one half of it was in green leaf
and the other half was burning from root to brilliant tip
where the wind raked sparks like seeds from its highest boughs.

/

A FARMER ON the island of Môn
jutting off the northwest tip of Wales
sometime in the eighteenth century

three times saw a ketch-rigged ship
fly through clouds over the Eryri mountains
into whose wide wastes we now drove.

Cloud drifted over crag vapours pooled in valleys
and the sun periodically struck through with sudden insight.
Everything was refracted by the damp air

so mountain peaks appeared as though through a lens
and vast cloud shadows constantly travelled across
the ever-changing landscape below the peaks.

In the early morning sun scattered through thin vapours
as I gazed at dark slag heaps raised like cinder cones
against the green-and-brown hills beyond

we passed Llyn Cwellyn's still slate-blue waters
and then arrived at our destination / Rhyd-ddu / a small valley village
from which Wordsworth was also supposed to have set off

in search of the universal spectacle. We parked in the grass
on the side of the narrow lane
the village little more than a handful of scattered houses and a pub

we heard a song thrush skylarks and a rook
and a red kite circled above as we set off
through some scrubby oaks and jumbled mossy stones

among which mangy sheep wandered.
The sheep it turned out would be everywhere in this landscape
it also turned out that my companions were far better climbers

so that I had a tendency to fall behind. K at least
kept me company. There were drystone walls tufts of wild grasses
and abandoned stone huts slumped against loose and tumbling crags.

Everything had the look of former activity
pits that might have been mines
ruined stone huts where shepherds perhaps once sheltered

a small angular patch of dark forest in the distance
could have been a spruce plantation
but mostly the open land was treeless

the living air quick to remove seed from sanctuary
and the open horizon thus making
all countries part of one single realm

and as we climbed higher small lakes and other mountains
came into view below and beyond
even the Irish Sea could eventually be glimpsed through a notch

clouds were moving in and the patchwork of tawny
green-purple light and dark brown-and-yellow earth
altered again and again as alternating cloud shadow

and direct sun moved quickly across the mutable
and glacially sculpted sweep of everything.
We hiked along the sharp edge of a horseshoe-shaped bite

below the peak like the crumbling lip of a volcano
with jagged stone teeth jutting up here and there
and Llyn Nadroedd a round mirror visible in the bowl deep below.

From here our path to the summit went right up over
a series of steep razorback crags the slopes of scree
sliding precipitously away on both sides of the narrow ridge.

K who did not care for such vertiginous prospects
moved slowly now her forehead bent earthward
and I was only too happy to creep along at this pace

but soon our path opened out towards the summit
and we gained the peak where the restaurant complex
clinging to the mountain against the wind

swarmed with tourists who had taken the small red-and-green train
and now fed the countless screeching gulls their unwanted chips.
We clambered down the eastern slope a short way

and found a quieter spot where our legs dangled off the precipice
with stunning views of Crib-y-Ddysgl and Y Lliwedd
and looking all the way south Cadair Idris.

We had our lunch which we had packed here
Eryri was a tiny patch of stark treeless mountains
and yet it felt like the heart of the true world

source of winds place where time turned on its subterranean wheel
allowing the sun to rise and set, the stars to spin about this still point
at the middle of everything else the dark material of the cosmos

gathered up in folds so all the valley quivered one extended motion
wind undulating on mossy hills a giant wash that sank
white fog delicately down red runnels on the mountainside

whose leaf–branch tendrils moved asway in granitic undertow
down and lifted the floating nebulous upward
and lifted the arms of the trees and lifted the grasses

in an instant in balance
and lifted the lambs to hold still and lifted the green of the hill
in one solemn wave.

Our descent took us due south
down through rapidly moving clouds
over scree and steep grassy slopes and along crumbling drystone walls

by the time we passed through an abandoned slate mine
between broken walls and heaps of shattered slate
the dark clouds had closed right in

the world become entirely black and white
and the rain finally came down turning the slates to mercury and steel
and in passing revealing tiny tender mosses

and flat green lichens on the ancient stones
and squall by squall the rain returned
drenching our final miles back to Rhyd-ddu

so the natural world fell
into the slow process of dissolution
into which we had driven it / a state of pure dementia

I thought then as I plodded along of the expanding universe
the four of us straggling along in the rain
each alone with our thoughts becoming more distant all the time

the surprise when astronomers found that not only
is the universe's flight away from itself not slowing
it is in fact accelerating heading perhaps towards a big rip

in which everything would finally be torn asunder.
We at last reached the village and dried ourselves out in the pub
until it was time for the drive back to Aberdesach

where we would arrive to watch the sun set over
the Irish Sea once again / brilliant crimson towards the Irish coast
though raining again lightly now over our beachhead

and as we turned back towards the cottage
I placed my hand wearily on J's shoulder
and looked up to see a ship in full sail high over the mountains.

/

MY FEET WERE shot my legs shot
I would not climb further this time
I left the others and took myself to Barmouth by train

where the jagged treeless peaks of the mountains rose
in almost fearful silhouette above gleaming slate roofs
silver willows and darker alder woods the fells tinged blue

and below / deep bosky thickets. There was something I needed
to recover from some gap or separation from something
to which I belonged but had no way of telling how

nor what I might even call it. Everything was fading
before our eyes into colours no one saw hidden in submarine gardens
or the deepest pools of lavender dew sentient marvels

oscillating between vegetable animal and mineral kingdoms.
Despite my fatigue the next day I could not stop myself from hobbling
across the Pont Abermaw the Mawddach beat up by the wind.

I was almost alone. The path on the far side followed
the tops of dikes among sheepfolds lined by wind-battered
bracken stunted foxglove and gorse clinging

amid the rock and slate skylarks hovered and buzzed
and I noted that the vagabonds growing beside my path
were themselves world-weary travellers / American beachgrass

lovely sweet vernal grass and spiny sea holly upon one of whose
bright lavender flowers a bee clung in the wind
as though a fixed and permanent part of its host plant.

Before me lay the village of Fairbourne low behind its berm
and broad sea defences from the top of which you could easily see
that the village on the one side and the sea on the other

were at best at the same level. Walk down the steep shingle
and the roofs of the village houses disappear / the sea
equally invisible but always audible from the village side too.

Rising sea levels mean Fairbourne is slated to be abandoned
and given back to the sea. I stood there in the battering wind
imagining a lost language of long-departed trees

still being whispered beneath the rough green sea
where its seeds shook under the waves and I then recalled
an elderly woman I once encountered at Covehithe on the Suffolk coast

where the sea steadily eats the land pointing down the path where
I'd come from the crumbling cliffs and saying "it's coming for us."
In the small gardens of Fairbourne's residents I noted hydrangeas

(from Asia) rhododendrons (from the Himalayas) devil's club
(most commonly from the Pacific Northwest coast of Canada) as well as
starlings and house sparrows who both have made

the whole world their mobile household.
Just above the village small fragments of ancient forest
clung to crevices / deep folds in the land

no human use had been found for / sharing the lower slopes
of coastal Eryri with a mix of other broadleaf trees
and a few large houses and the scar of an abandoned slate mine.

Between these lower woods and the towering bare sheepscape
of seashell-shaped peaks above, from which the ancient trees
of what was once rainforest had departed so long ago departed

that it's forgotten they were ever there
a phalanx of plantation spruce march with their monocultural wounds
in dark orderly ranks over a ridge in the middle of things.

They are not here of their own accord / no being out of place
is actually ever a being out of place so long as they can root into the
earth / however thin it may be however temporary however despised

these Sitka spruce may be as "foreign interlopers"
each and every one an immutable traveller their seeds
sent as emissaries in pursuit of climates that have since outpaced them

only our language of belonging lags behind
tripped up by species' borders
unaware that breath is a tree's most intimate gradient too.

I imagined taking myself into those cool dark spruces
see the sacred forests and the flame of growth blaze
find there a lovely dense living forest its branches trembling bent and

bowed together in that perpetual shade that reformed *selva antica*
finding diasporic solace among the close columns
seeking a kind of welcoming from long-lost friends and relatives

fellow castaways on this archipelago earth
marooned colonies of the forcibly displaced collateral damage
of capital and a deep ignorance of ecological mobility

who can impress the forest bid the tree
unfix its earthbound root? I imagined a garden where
everything was in motion the plants coming and going as they would

the expansive thrust and flux of life unimpeded by human reorderings
interacting without borders / such gardens would be more like neurons
in a cerebral canopy firing in response to one another forming temporary

spatial relations / undocumented thoughtways / vagabond ideas
of a mobile music. Not only species we consider invasive but most plants
we think of as having always been in a particular place are actually

migrants from a more or less distant past: the "invasive" plant of today
is the "native" flora of the future / I warmly greet these *flora non grata*
seeds are survival capsules transporting vegetable life in space and time

let us sing their heroic exploits / every living being is part
of a network of relationships about which we know almost nothing
I had to imagine the trees were mustering for battle once again

I was a glitch in time and space / a text cut out of other texts
I was a universe of orphaned shards / tinder in fires sweeping hillsides
I was a raindrop in the atmosphere of rivers / a bubble on the swollen stream

so saying I turned limping back towards Barmouth
recalling then that Darwin had been here too on geological tour
confirming that the high sheepwrecked peaks had once been sea bottom

on a summit strewed with boulders of foreign rock
I found rounded chalk flints / the drift of these counties
thus admitting their submarine origins. Ours

are a million aimless journeys through shifting climates
mobile gardens of song where we carry seeds into dispersal
a beyondery we are forever yearning towards

the outside of the plantation we inevitably escape
trees fleeing through the night where I recall Osman /
Eritrean Odysseus / his hands held out cupped one over the other

opens them and reveals a white moth slowly moving
its wings / flower of the palest *lavendula* species
willow bridge snow or silver ghost

Osman lifts his hands
and we laugh as it blows / flies away
as the Planetary Garden slowly shifts the address of paradise

/

FROM SOMEWHERE OVER the Atlantic
I remembered a last glimpse of what I thought Wales to be
from the car window as we turned into a mountain valley

the sky obliterated by western light
diffused through Turneresque vapour
and beyond the last silhouette of hill

a body of water towering lighthouse sailboat and mountains
recalling for me Blake's drawing
of Dante's Stygian Lake in Canto VII of the *Inferno*.

I wondered who I was outside of the pattern of movements
I inscribed over the face of the earth
as what I thought I was fled when I came too close.

My flight was one of those
afternoon-through-evening crossings west that seemed
to chase and prolong the sunset

a glitch drawn out across the surface of the sphere
like an extended note long in fading
at the close of a lengthy piece of music.

The time had come to set out on my journey westward
but it was always a longer journey than I expected
and yet again always over more quickly than you would have thought

my mind hovering over the geometry
of the arcing line across this gentle globe
which the screen in front of me demonstrated again and again.

I thought of the Sitka spruce standing tall and breathing
out fragrances on the very farthest edge of my westward flight
pictured it in my mind when last I saw it

struck golden by the setting sun as we made our way
back to our campsite and recalled too the buzzing of bees
I stood and listened to there once

wondering if the hive was up there in the spruce's ample canopy.
Thus in my mind I entered the architecture of bees / the gold of their
mossed bodies recalling to me Karl Von Frisch's

The Dance Language and Orientation of Bees where
the ethologist watched bees dancing before the face of the honeycomb
analyzed their choreographic syntax and articulated their vocabulary.

When a bee finds a source of food
it returns to the hive and communicates the distance
and direction of the food to the other bees.

The bee starts by making a short straight run
wobbling side to side and buzzing as it goes
then it turns and walks in a semicircle back to the starting point

the bee then repeats the short run down the middle
makes a semicircle to the opposite side
and returns once again to the starting point.

If you draw a line connecting the beehive and the food source
and another line connecting the hive
and the spot on the horizon just beneath the sun

the angle formed by the two lines is the same
as the angle of the bee's wobbling run to the imaginary vertical line:
bees it appears are able to triangulate as well as a civil engineer.

But how does the bee do this? How does this tiny animal
with its miniature brain encode so much detailed
quantitative information in the abstract language of its dance?

Barbara Shipman found out using the esoteric mathematics of flag manifolds.
A manifold is a shape of some kind / a surface
that geometric patterns specific to the shape can be plotted upon.

A flag manifold has six dimensions / an imaginary form
theoreticians love to fiddle with and which I do not pretend to understand.
The easiest way to visualize objects that have more than three dimensions

is to map them onto a surface with fewer dimensions
project a six-dimensional flag manifold onto a two-dimensional surface
and you get a hexagon as in a honeycomb.

Certain geometric patterns particular to the six-dimensional
flag manifold when projected onto the two-dimensional hexagon
match the pattern danced by bees.

Six-dimensional flag manifolds are also used by physicists
in the quantum mathematics associated with quarks
the tiny building blocks of protons and neutrons.

Shipman suggests the physics of bees' bodies
must be constructed such that
they are sensitive to quantum fields

the bee perceives these fields through
quantum mechanical interactions between the fields
and the atoms in the membranes of certain of its cells.

Perhaps bees possess some ability
to perceive not only light and magnetism
but quarks and even quantum fields.

The closer we look the less we understand
the more there is yet to be discovered
more and more it seems

only human beings are ignorant enough
to engineer their own destruction
to make a method of cutting each other off

ensuring their mutual subjection and dissolution
by and large through cutting themselves off
from all other species as well. I could not read.

I merely stared at the flight map
watching the spherical world turn in faux three dimensions
the track of my flight arc again and again over the surface of the globe

the continuous image of the poetic condition outlining a mountain
I am still on that mountain round which souls spiral upward keening
lost in mists and moving cloud and the dreams of missing trees.

Do we not see the path of the wind and the rain?
Do we not see the oaks beating together?
Do we not see the sea scouring the coastline?

Do we not see the sun sailing the heavens like a ship?
Do we not see the darkness trailing behind?
Do we not see that the stars have fallen into the sea?

Do we not see the creatures taken back into the depths of the earth?
Do we not see the names of trees receding?
Do we not see that time has stopped stopping and bends towards the light?

Do we not see we have opened the door we were not to open?
Do we not see the seed of love the apple and the oar?
Do we not see the trees alive lying on the earth
     their shadows standing tall / trembling with fire and language?

Detail from William Blake, *Dante and Statius Sleeping, Virgil Watching* (illustration to
the *Divine Comedy*, Purgatorio XXVII) © Ashmolean Museum

NOTES

Many sources inspired, were consulted, or are cited in *The Middle* – the book is arguably *about* citation in many ways, although three very different practices are at work. In "Sketch of a Poem," citations are marked in italics; virtually all of "The Middle" is worked up out of various translations of Dante's *Purgatorio*; and the many citations in "Gardens in Motion" are largely unmarked, although they are listed here in these notes. This last poem owes much to W.G. Sebald, whose own work incorporated unmarked citations. If there is a phytopoetics at work in *The Middle*, it is one of seed dispersal, where certain words (often the names of trees) move across the book, but it may also be discernable in the fact that the citations in the book's first section are more easily identifiable *as* citations (newly planted on cleared ground), while by the book's last section what is cited has been swallowed by the surging and resurgent garden in motion. This may itself suggest a sort of rewilding of the poem's citational method.

To cite in poetry, I have believed, is to participate in the commons that poetry exhibits better than any other genre: our literary resources are shared, a common treasury for all. Citation may also be a form of solidarity. But I am compelled to note my sources here because, as Fady Joudah has said, "There is a solidarity whose horizon is assimilation, and there is a solidarity whose horizon is liberation. The former is hierarchical to those it is in solidarity with. The latter is in community with them. The former treats them as abstraction. The latter is citational. It names those it loves" (*The New Inquiry*). I would name what I love, and be in community with the many writers whose work I gratefully take up here.

Opening epigraphs: Etel Adnan, "The Spring Flowers Own," *The Spring Flowers Own and The Manifestations of the Voyage*; The Pretenders, "Middle of the Road," *Learning to Crawl*; Samuel Beckett, quoted in Deirdre Bair, *Samuel Beckett: A Biography*.

Preface

Epigraph: Jenny Erpenbeck, "There's a Time in Life When You Need to Read Hermann Hesse," *Guardian*.

Robert Pogue Harrison, "Labors of Love" (*New York Review of Books*); Dante Alighieri, *Purgatorio* (trans. D.M. Black); Teodolinda Barolini, *The Undivine Comedy: Detheologizing Dante*; Jacques Le Goff, *The Birth of Purgatory* (trans. Arthur Goldhammer); Vivek Narayanan, *After*; Stephano Mancuso, *The Incredible Journey of Plants*; Louis F. Pitelka and the Plant Migration Workshop Group, "Plant Migration and Climate Change: A More Realistic Portrait of Plant Migration Is Essential to Predicting Biological Responses to Global Warming in a World Drastically Altered by Human Activity" (*American Scientist*); Gilles Clément, "The Planetary Garden" and Other Writings (trans. Sandra Morris), "Manifesto of the Third Landscape" (trans. Europe Halles), and "In Praise of Vagabonds," (trans. Jonathan Skinner, *Qui Parle*); Jonathan Skinner, "Gardens of Resistance: Gilles Clément, New Poetics, and Future Landscapes" (*Qui Parle*).

Sketch of a Poem I Will Not Have Written: A Blazing Space

Epigraph: annie ross, "how to talk to more-than-humans," *Some People Fall in the Lodge and Then Eat Berries All Winter*.

First Movement: Robin Blaser, *Bach's Belief* and *The Holy Forest*; Ronald Johnson, *The Book of the Green Man*; Homer, *The Iliad* (trans. Emily Wilson).

Second Movement: Etel Adnan, *Time* (trans. Sarah Riggs); Gaston Bachelard, *The Psychoanalysis of Fire* (trans. Alan C.M. Ross); Robin

Blaser, *The Holy Forest*; Fady Joudah, *Tethered to Stars*; John Vaillant, *Fire Weather*; Phyllis Webb, *Peacock Blue: The Collected Poems*; Homer, *The Iliad* (trans. Emily Wilson).

Third Movement: Hannah Arendt, *Essays in Understanding, 1930–1954: Formation, Exile, and Totalitarianism*; H.D., *The Walls Do Not Fall* and *Tribute to the Angels*; Isabella Wang, *Pebble Swing*.

Fourth Movement: Dante Alighieri, *Convivio* (trans. Andrew Frisardi); Édouard Glissant, *The Poetics of Relation* (trans. Betsy Wing); Susan Howe, *Spontaneous Particulars: The Telepathy of Archives*; Jacques Le Goff, *The Birth of Purgatory* (trans. Arthur Goldhammer); Talking Heads, "This Must Be the Place (Naive Melody)," *Speaking in Tongues*.

Fifth Movement: Robin Blaser, *The Holy Forest*; Michael Hamburger, *Sebald. Orte*; Robert Pogue Harrison, *Forests: The Shadow of Civilization*; Friedrich Hölderlin, *Hymns and Fragments* (trans. Richard Sieburth); Ronald Johnson, *The Book of the Green Man*; Ilya Kaminsky, *Deaf Republic*; Federico Garcia Lorca, *Collected Poems* (trans. Christopher Maurer); Cecily Nicholson, *From the Poplars*; Nathaniel Tarn, *The Hölderliniae*; Phyllis Webb, *Peacock Blue: The Collected Poems*.

The Middle

Epigraphs: Abdulrazak Gurnah, *Refugee Tales*; Friedrich Hölderlin, "Patmos," *Hymns and Fragments* (trans. Richard Sieburth).

Dante Alighieri, *Purgatorio* (trans. D.M. Black and trans. W.S. Merwin).

Gardens in Motion

Epigraphs: Inger Christensen, "The Regulating Effect of Chance," *The Condition of Secrecy*, (trans. Susanna Nied).

William Blake, *The Marriage of Heaven and Hell*; Paco Calvo with Natalie Lawrence, *Planta Sapiens: The New Science of Plant Intelligence*; Robin Blaser, *The Holy Forest*; Gilles Clément, *"The Planetary Garden" and Other Writings* (trans. Sandra Morris); Dante Alighieri, *Purgatorio* (trans. D.M. Black); Charles Darwin, *The Life and Letters of Charles Darwin* (ed. Francis Darwin); Adam Frank, "Quantum Honeybees"; Evan C. Fricke et al., "The Effects of Defaunation on Plants' Capacity to Track Climate Change"; Paul Friedrich, *Proto-Indo-European Trees: The Arboreal System of a Prehistoric People*; Allen Ginsberg, "Wales Visitation," *Collected Poems 1947–1997*; Édouard Glissant, *The Poetics of Relation* (trans. Betsy Wing); Robert Graves, *The White Goddess: a Historical Grammar of Poetic Myth*; Jean-Francois Le Galliard et al., "Dispersal and Range Dynamics in Changing Climates: A Review"; Robert Pogue Harrison, *Forests: The Shadow of Civilization*; Friedrich Hölderlin, *Hymns and Fragments* (trans. Richard Sieburth); Peter Larkin, *If Trees Allay an Earth Retrialling*; Ronald Johnson, *The Book of the Green Man*; Federico Garcia Lorca, *Suites* (trans. Jerome Rothenberg); Stefano Mancuso, *The Incredible Journeys of Plants*; Jan Morris, *Wales: Epic Views of a Small Country*; Ran Nathan et al., "A Movement Ecology Paradigm for Unifying Organismal Movement Research"; Ronald P. Neilson et al., "Forecasting Regional to Global Plant Migration in Response to Climate Change"; Richard G. Pearson, "Climate Change and the Migration Capacity of Species"; Gretta T. Pecl et al., "Biodiversity Redistribution under Climate Change: Impacts on Ecosystems and Human Well-Being"; Louis F. Pitelka and the Plant Migration Workshop Group, "Plant Migration and Climate Change"; Oliver Rackham, *Woodlands*; W.G. Sebald, *Austerlitz* (trans. Anthea Bell); William Shakespeare, *Macbeth*; Guy Shrubsole, *The Lost Rainforests of Britain*; Zach St. George, *The Journeys of Trees: A Story about Forests, People, and the Future*; Philippe Sollers, as cited in Blaser's "Great Companion: Dante Alighiere"; *The Book of Taliesin: Poems of Warfare and Praise in an Enchanted Britain* (trans. Gwyneth Lewis and Rowan Williams); William Wordsworth, "Lines Composed a Few Miles Above Tintern Abbey" and *The Prelude*; Homer, *The Odyssey* (trans. A.T. Murray).

ACKNOWLEDGMENTS

Poetry from *The Middle*, often in very different form, has appeared in *etcetera*, *the scales project*, the Richler Library *Shelf Portraits: Inside the Libraries of Canadian Authors*, *Send My Love to Anyone*, and in two chapbooks: *Blazing Space* (Muscaliet Press, 2022) and *Gardens in Motion* (above/ground, 2023). A version of the preface was delivered as a talk at Simon Fraser University in April of 2023 and subsequently published in *The Goose* as "The Middle of the Middle: Purgatory, Pilgrimage, and Human and Plant Mobility in a Time of Climate Crisis." Thanks to the editors.

Thanks to my readers David Herd and Catriona Strang for comments and encouragement.

Thanks to Isabella Wang for an exchange of poems in the wake of Phyllis Webb's passing, to Tony Power for assistance with Robin Blaser's books, to Cecily Nicholson for endless walks and talks, to Elee Kraljii Gardiner for asking what is in the middle of the middle, and to Ted Byrne for conversations on Dante. Thanks to Jonathan Skinner for turning me on to (and for his translations of) Gilles Clément, and to Jonathan, Katherine Zeltner, Patrick Barron, and Nick Lawrence for our Snowdonian adventure. Thanks to Kaie Kellough for a reminder of this Lisa Robertson passage, a ghost epigraph found after the fact: "From now on, everything will be called The Middle" (*3 Summers*).

Thanks to everyone at Talon, thanks to Cathy, Sophie, Hannah, and Josh, and thanks to Anna Pincus and my Refugee Tales family as well.

Stephen Collis is the author of over a dozen books of poetry and prose, including *The Commons* (2008), *On the Material* (2010), winner of the BC Book Prize, and *Almost Islands: Phyllis Webb and the Pursuit of the Unwritten* (2018) – all published by Talonbooks. *A History of the Theories of Rain* (2021) was a finalist for the Governor General's Award for Poetry, and in 2019 Collis was the recipient of the Writers' Trust of Canada Latner Poetry Prize. *The Middle* is the second volume of a trilogy begun with *A History of the Theories of Rain*. He lives near Vancouver, on unceded Coast Salish Territory, and teaches poetry and poetics at Simon Fraser University.

PHOTO: Stephen Collis